Contents

Units

1. **The Sort of Person I Am** — 2
   Personal descriptions
2. **Ideas for Stories** — 4
   Fiction
3. **Points of View** — 6
   Reports of events
4. **Weird Creatures** — 8
   Prose descriptions
5. **A Bird Poem in the Making** — 10
   Poetic descriptions, drafting
6. **Ideas for Poems** — 12
   Poetic descriptions
7. **Memories** — 14
   Poems
8. **The Story of My Life** — 15
   Autobiographical writing
9. **Planning a Party** — 16
   Plans, invitations
10. **Starting a Story** — 18
    Fiction
11. **Jumbie Stories** — 20
    Regional dialects
12. **Naming Things** — 22
    Language variation
13. **The Diver** — 24
    Prose descriptions
14. **Riddles** — 26
    Contrived descriptions
15. **Bats' Teeth** — 28
    Poetic descriptions
16. **Rules of the Game** — 30
    Instructions
17. **What Do You Think?** — 32
    Letter writing
18. **The Prayer of the Little Ducks** — 34
    Prayers
19. **Daydreams** — 35
    Descriptive poetry
20. **Paragraphs** — 36
    Fiction
21. **Choose a Character** — 38
    Fiction
22. **Book Reviews** — 40
    Description and evaluation
23. **New Fantastic Chocochips** — 42
    Slogans and rhymes
24. **Slang** — 44
    Standard and non-standard English
25. **Crazy Machines** — 46
    Descriptions and designs
26. **Who'll Look After Us?** — 48
    Fiction
27. **A Map of the Feelings** — 50
    Descriptive poetry
28. **Myself and Other People** — 52
    Autobiographical writing
29. **Survival** — 54
    Instructions
30. **The Captain's Diary** — 56
    Fictional diaries
31. **The Loch Ness Monster** — 58
    Long stories
32. **School Newspapers** — 60
    Producing a newspaper
33. **Writing for Little Children** — 62
    Picture books

The Sort of Person I Am

 Read these children's descriptions of themselves. Are you like any of them? In what ways are you different?

The things I enjoy doing most are going off to the park and chatting to my friend Alison. At home I like looking after our rabbit Bouncer and letting him sit on my lap. He sniffs in and out very fast and tries to put his nose in my pocket. But I hate cleaning out his cage.

The rest of the time I like reading and listening to cassettes in my bedroom where my brother can't come in and bother me.

Suria (10)

I think that the worst thing you can do is carry out experiments on animals.

Experiments on animals are wrong because innocent creatures are often permanently injured and have parts of their bodies removed.

I know that doctors have to try out their new medicines to make sure they work. They also have to discover how the body works. If they didn't do this they might make mistakes when we go into hospital.

But I think the doctors should do these experiments on each other, not on animals. Then they would have to be much more careful.

The next worst is not looking after old people and making them live in homes. The third worst is smoking because it ruins your health and makes your breath stink.

Paul (10)

When I am older I would like to become a journalist on a newspaper. I'm good at describing things I've seen and I'd like to interview famous people. But I would not like visiting the scene of an accident. And I'll have to improve my spelling.

Odette (10)

At school I like writing stories but only if I've got a good idea for one. I hate simply being told to 'write a story' without any suggestions for what it can be about. I also like writing poems as long as we don't have to make them rhyme.

Jason (11)

Write a description of yourself, so that the person who reads it will know what you are really like. Write the title The Sort of Person I Am.

You can begin I enjoy... (You can describe games, books, lessons, TV programmes, holidays etc.)

You can go on I think... (Tell us what you dislike or disagree with as Paul did. Explain why.)

You can go on When I am older...

And finish with At school I like... (Tell us what lessons you like or find difficult. Explain what sort of writing you like doing.)

Ideas for Stories

Authors get ideas for stories from a variety of different sources. Some begin by thinking of a **character** and they build a story round him or her. Others think of an unusual **happening** or a **title**. Sometimes they begin with an interesting **opening sentence** and simply see where it takes them to. Which sort of starting point do you find most helpful?

1 Characters

Here are some characters for you to write about. First choose one, then think of a **name** for him or her. Then think of the sort of things that your character might do.

2 What if . . .

What would happen if there was a plant which started to grow and grow and grow?

What would happen if you (or somebody else) were a brilliant inventor and could make something amazing?

What would happen if you were swimming in the sea and saw, underneath the water, people living amidst the rocks? You could call your story *The Kingdom Under the Sea.*

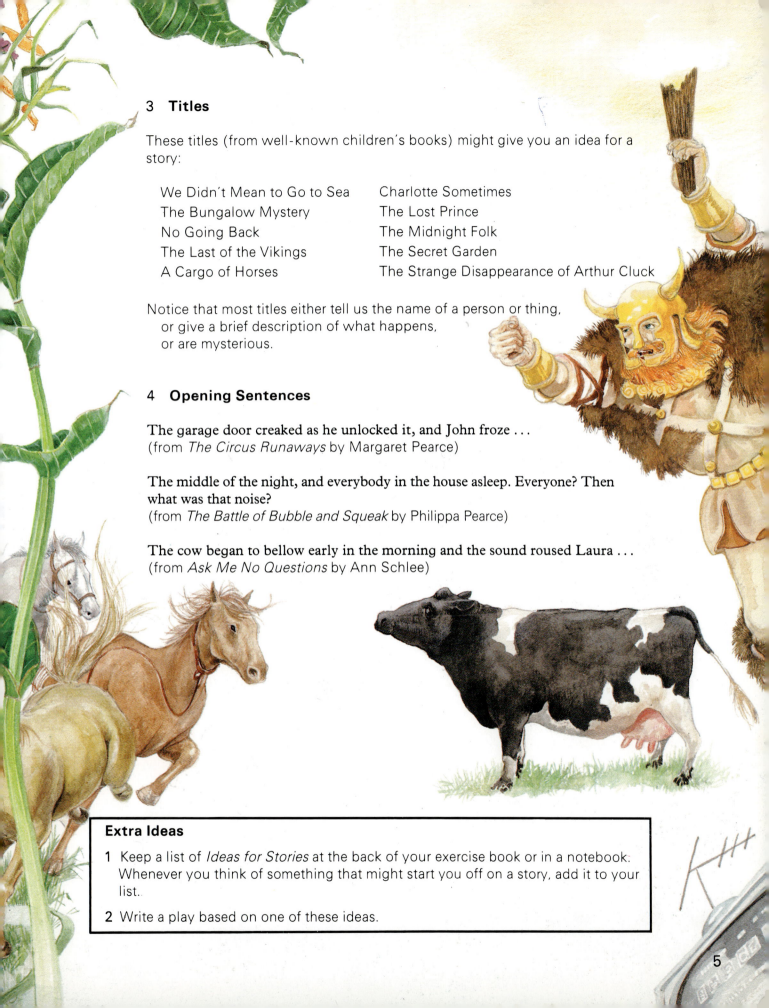

3 Titles

These titles (from well-known children's books) might give you an idea for a story:

We Didn't Mean to Go to Sea
The Bungalow Mystery
No Going Back
The Last of the Vikings
A Cargo of Horses

Charlotte Sometimes
The Lost Prince
The Midnight Folk
The Secret Garden
The Strange Disappearance of Arthur Cluck

Notice that most titles either tell us the name of a person or thing,
or give a brief description of what happens,
or are mysterious.

4 Opening Sentences

The garage door creaked as he unlocked it, and John froze …
(from *The Circus Runaways* by Margaret Pearce)

The middle of the night, and everybody in the house asleep. Everyone? Then what was that noise?
(from *The Battle of Bubble and Squeak* by Philippa Pearce)

The cow began to bellow early in the morning and the sound roused Laura …
(from *Ask Me No Questions* by Ann Schlee)

Extra Ideas

1 Keep a list of *Ideas for Stories* at the back of your exercise book or in a notebook. Whenever you think of something that might start you off on a story, add it to your list.

2 Write a play based on one of these ideas.

Read this lady's account of what happened to her:

I'd been shopping all the morning and was tired out. My little boy kept whining "Can't we go home now?"

Suddenly we heard people shouting and cars hooting. Then a red van came hurtling down the hill. I felt the wind on my face as it rushed past! I was so shocked I dropped my shopping and there were broken eggs and yoghurts and tomatoes all over the pavement.

Then I heard a loud bump followed by a noise like a thousand matchboxes being crumpled up, and everybody was shouting. The van was stuck through a fence! I think its brakes must have failed or the driver fell asleep. Thank goodness nobody seemed to be hurt.

The lady has written this entirely from her own **point of view**. She tells us only what *she* saw and thought.

Now you write about it from some of the other people's points of view.

1 Write the heading The Driver's Point of View. Describe it as he would have done, explaining how he felt as his brakes started to fail, what it was like crashing into things, and how he feels now. You might begin I left the factory this morning at...

2 Write the heading The Vegetable Seller's Point of View and describe it as he would have done. He is probably upset about his fruit and vegetables. You might begin I was just serving onions to...

3 Write what you think the driver's boss had to say when he heard about it.

Extra Ideas

Write what you think the driver's wife said when she heard about it.

Write an account of what happened for the local newspaper.

Weird Creatures

Read this description of a **porcelain crab**. The writer has tried to explain exactly what it looks like. He also shows how he *feels* about it.

It is entirely covered in thin bone which is hard and shiny like beautiful china. It has a great round head with two little round eyes. It reminds me of a ghostly human face. It doesn't seem to have any body.

Two large curved arms grow out of the side of its head with a pair of savage looking claws on each end. They remind me of the beak of a fierce eagle. Further up its head, six more thin arms grow. Perhaps they help it to walk.

I'm glad it is only 2 cm long. If it were much bigger, I would keep well clear of it!

 Which sentences in this description tell us what it really looks like?
Which sentences tell us what the reader thinks and feels?

First Drafts

You make first drafts so that it won't matter if you make mistakes or alterations or move text around.

You can make as many crossings out as you like.

The handwriting doesn't matter as long as you can read it yourself.

When you have finished, *check it over* to make sure that it is exactly as you want it to be. Check the spellings.

Then copy it out in your best handwriting.

Choose one or more of these weird creatures and write about it. Describe exactly what it looks like and also how you feel about it.

Make a draft copy of it first so that you can make alterations and improvements.

Moles live in long tunnels under fields and lawns throughout Britain. They are about 12 centimetres long.

Bats roost in caves and deserted buildings in the day time. They fly out at night to hunt insects. Their wingspan is usually about 20 centimetres.

Daddy-long-legs have legs about 4 centimetres long. They often fly indoors in the summer and get caught in lampshades and spiders' webs.

Extra Ideas

1 Think of any other creature that you have actually seen. Draw and describe it accurately. You can choose a quite ordinary one such as a cat or a goldfish or an insect.

2 Invent a new creature. Draw it, give it a name and describe it.

3 You could convert one of your descriptions into a poem.

A Bird Poem in the Making

A boy called Soloman wrote a poem called *Birds*. This is how he did it.

Stage one – first draft

He made a draft copy. He kept crossing out words he didn't like and altering bits.

Stage two – revising

He read it out to his teacher and his friends. They suggested some improvements. He agreed with some of their ideas but not all of them.

"You said swoops twice," said Sadia.

"All right, I'll say sliding the second time," said Soloman and altered his rough copy.

Matthew said, "I think it ends too suddenly. What happened to the fish?"

Everyone had ideas: "It wriggles … it squirms … it struggles … it trembles …"

"I like It wriggles in despair," said Soloman and again altered his rough copy.

Stage three

He copied it out adding some final improvements that he had thought of.

What do you think of the last sentence?

Birds

The eagle swoops along the river sliding in and out of trees.
Like a blur of gold.
It sees a fish like a crocodile
It swoops down.
Suddenly it dives into the water
It picks up the fish with it's huge claws like a pair of giant's hands.
The fish wrigles in despair.

Soloman Nicholson

See the next two pages for some ideas for writing poems of your own.

Ideas for Poems

Choose one of the topics on these two pages to write a poem.

First, make a list of ideas for your poem.

Then start your draft copy, describing each thing exactly.

Go over your draft copy crossing out and improving the parts you don't like, making it as clear and interesting as you can.

Copy it out carefully in your best handwriting.

Playground Life

What do people do in the playground?

What noises do you hear?

What do people shout?

What do they whisper?

What else do you notice?

What do you feel or think as you watch the others?

It's Raining!

What do you say when it's raining?

What do you see as you look out of the window?

If you go out, what do you notice?

What do you feel?

What do you hear?

What do you say as you come back indoors?

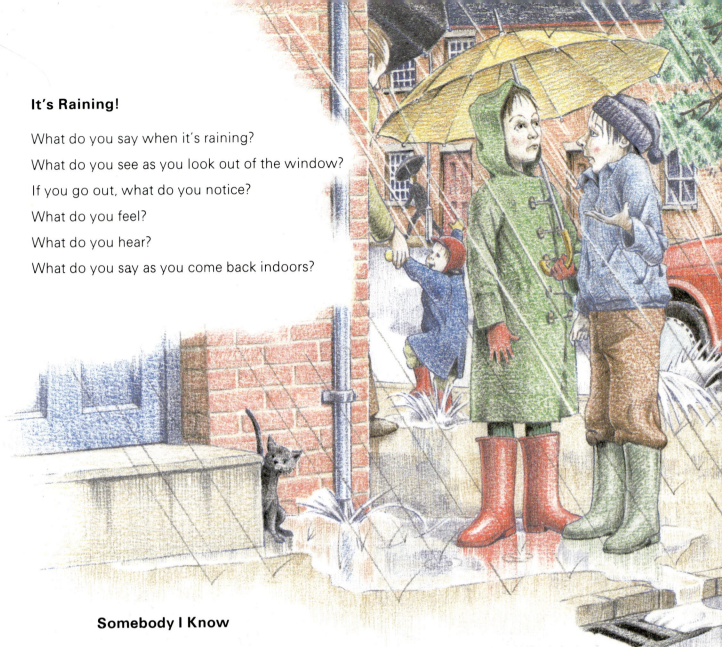

Somebody I Know

Think of somebody you know well; it could be a relation or a friend (or even a pet). Note down any special things you notice about him or her – appearance, habits, ways of talking, likes and dislikes ...

How do you feel about the person at different times? Do you sometimes get angry or amused or loving or sad? Why?

When you have made plenty of notes, pick out the interesting words and sentences to make a poem.

Rhyming

Your poems will be much better if they don't rhyme.

If you do try to make them rhyme it will be very difficult to say exactly what you mean.

Memories

One, chubby little cheeks and a pink dummy.
Two, splattering baby food in my high chair.
Three, walking down the street singing to myself.
Four, starting school, Mrs Camburn took us to the zoo.
Five, Graham Queen trying to strangle me in the playground.
Six, every morning before work saying our prayers.
Seventh birthday party, a gigantic cake, puffing at the candles.
Eight, the house upstairs blazing red and orange bright flames.
My dad dying when I was *nine*.
Ten, waving mum goodbye as we set off for Wales.

Annette (10)

 What do you remember best about when you were very young? Do you have memories of parties, Christmas, outings, things at home, visits to hospital, happy, sad or exciting moments?

Draw three pictures of yourself when you were one, six and now.

One, in my cot.

Six, fighting and kicking and pulling my cousin Jane's hair out.

Ten, in Wales, disco dancing with Ruth.

Now write a poem for the years one to ten as Annette did above.

First make notes: jot down one memory for each year. Close your eyes and try to remember. (You can imagine the sorts of things you did when you were one.)

The Story of My Life

Do some research at home. Ask your parents these questions and make some notes from their answers:

Where exactly were you born?

Why did they choose your name?

Did they have any other ideas about what to call you?

Were you a good baby? Did you do anything naughty or funny?

  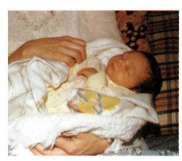 

Write The Story of My Life. Use the things your parents told you and your own memories to **write your autobiography**, describing all the things that have ever happened to you. (Include your favourite toys or friends, nice holidays, any accidents and your first day at school.)

My name is Michael David Barnes. This me as a baby. My birthday is on May 8th.

Gary and me at the seaside. I was about 7 years old.

I was about 3 years old here. My brother Gary is the silly one. We were in the garden with some friends.

Mum and Dad took me out for a special treat on my 10th birthday.

Planning a Party

Imagine you can give a party – any sort of party you like! Money is no problem.

1 In rough, make plans for the best party there has ever been.

Your notes should help you to answer all these questions:

What day will your party be? What time?

Where will it be? (You can hire a restaurant, or hall, or boat, or go to the seaside.)

Who will you invite? (You can ask pop stars, TV or sports personalities, the Royal Family – anyone, as well as your own friends.)

What will you eat and drink?

Do you want to hire a disco or an entertainer?

Will you have games and prizes? Will it be fancy dress?

Will you need any rules to stop people misbehaving?

Sunday ~~morning~~ afternoon
in the garden?

barbecue?   Paul ~~Ruth~~ Kim Alec
Coke   Paran Philip Schofield Princess Diana
Ribena   Liz McColgan   Mr Smith from
                                the sweetshop
~~Acrobat~~   ~~Hamburgers~~ ~~Crisps~~ rhubarb pie
Hire a video   Roast turkey   mangoes
Football   jaffa cakes roast potatoes hazelnut
                                            ice cream

2. Now write out your plans **neatly** for other people to read. They can be like this:

My Party Plan

Time and place: _____

People to invite: _____

Food and drink: _____

Entertainments and music: _____

Dress: _____

Rules to be kept: _____

Other things to remember: _____

3. Design a beautiful **invitation card** to send to people. Remember to include the time and place.

Extra Idea

Describe the party as if it really happened. Was it fun? You can describe the guests arriving. What did they wear? Who did they talk to? What did they most enjoy? Did anything go wrong?

Starting a Story

The opening sentence of a story is the hardest part to write. Read how these famous authors began their stories.

1 Starting with a conversation.

"Where's Papa going with that axe?" said Fern to her mother as they were setting the table for breakfast.

"Out to the hoghouse," replied Mrs Arable. "Some pigs were born last night."

"I don't see why he needs an axe," continued Fern, who was only eight.

"Well," said her mother, "one of the pigs is a runt. It's very small and weak, and it will never amount to anything. So your father has decided to do away with it."

"Do *away* with it?" shrieked Fern. "You mean *kill* it? Just because it's smaller than the others?"

Mrs Arable put a pitcher of cream on the table. "Don't yell, Fern!" she said. "Your father is right. The pig would probably die anyway."

Fern pushed a chair out of the way, and ran outdoors.

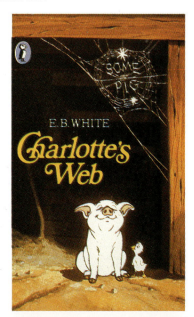

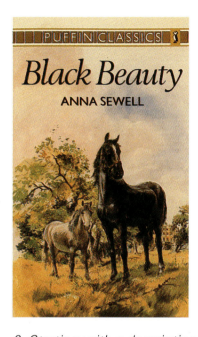

2 Starting with a description of a place.

The first place that I can well remember was a large pleasant meadow with a pond of clear water in it. Some shady trees leaned over it, and rushes and water-lilies grew at the deep end. Over the hedge on one side we looked into a ploughed field, and on the other we looked over a gate at our master's house, which stood by the road-side; at the top of the meadow was a plantation of fir trees, and at the bottom a running brook overhung by a steep bank.

Whilst I was young I lived upon my mother's milk, as I could not eat grass. In the day time I ran by her side, and at night I lay down close by her. When it was hot, we used to stand by the pond in the shade of the trees, . . .

3 Starting by introducing a character.

Granny Smith, an ordinary, little, old white-haired lady, resting on a seat in a public park, began to feel decidedly peculiar ...

Granny Smith was old and her eyesight and hearing were not as good as they used to be ...

Her arms were so frail that she couldn't even carry the lightest shopping bag, so she used a shopping trolley. And she *so* hated being seen with it – she said it made her look old!

Suddenly ... a beam of blue light shot out of nowhere, it seemed, and struck the little old lady.

4 Starting mysteriously with a simple sentence followed by questions.

The Iron Man came to the top of the cliff. How far had he walked? Nobody knew. Where had he come from? Nobody knew. How was he made? Nobody knew.

Taller than a house, the Iron Man stood at the top of the cliff, on the very brink, in the darkness.

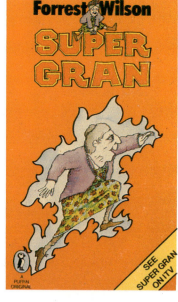
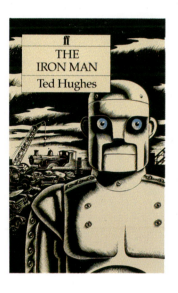

Which of these beginnings of stories do you like best? Which make you want to read on? Why?

Now **you** think of an idea for a story. The suggestions on pages 4 and 5 might help you. Then **draft out four different ways of starting the story**, like this:

1 **Start a conversation.** Think of *one or two* surprising things that somebody might say which could set your story going.

2 **Start with a place.** Think of any place (your house, a park, somewhere you have visited) and write *one or two* sentences about it which might then turn into a story.

3 **Introduce a character.** Write *one or two* sentences describing anybody you can think of, who might then become a character in a story.

4 **Start mysteriously** with some questions.

Then decide which of them to continue into a complete story.

19

Jumbie Stories

 Can you understand what these people are saying?

Marie lives in Glasgow.
She speaks in a **Scottish** dialect.

Tony lives near Newcastle.
People say he talks **Geordie**.

Gordon lives in London.
People say he speaks **Cockney**.

Grace's family came to England
from the **Caribbean**.

English is spoken differently in different areas. We call the special words and phrases of a particular area a **dialect**. The formal English you normally see in books is called **Standard English**.

 Do you know any dialect words from the area where you live? Make a list of them.

Can you explain why there might be a problem if dialect was used:
- in science or history books;
- on TV news programmes;
- in applications for office jobs?

Do you think it matters if people use dialect:
- chatting to friends;
- in a poem;
- in conversation in stories?

Grace Nichols grew up in Guyana, where they speak a form of West Indian dialect. Read this poem about listening to 'jumbie' stories – the local phrase for *ghost* stories.

I Like to Stay Up

I like to stay up
and listen
when big people talking
jumbie stories

OoooooooooH
I does feel so tingly
and excited
inside me

But when my mother say
'Girl, time for bed'
then is when
I does feel a dread
then is when
I does jump into me bed
then is when I does cover up
from me feet to me head

then is when
I does wish
I didn't listen
to no stupid jumbie story
then is when
I does wish
I did read me book instead

Grace Nichols

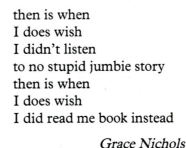

If you were reading the poem aloud, what tone of voice would you use for the second verse? Now read the whole poem, making it as lively as you can.

Pick out the words and phrases that are in dialect.

Next time you write a story, include a character who speaks in a special dialect.

Naming Things

 Have you ever thought how plants and creatures get their names? There are more than a million different sorts of creature and even more sorts of plants – and names had to be invented for them all!

Some plants have several different names:

The Wild Rose is called Pig's Rose in Devon, and Dog Rose in many other places. Its berries or hips are called Itching Berries in Lancashire, Choops in Cumbria, Nippernails in Cheshire, Pig's Noses in Devon, Pixie Pears in Hampshire and Soldiers in Kent. Which name do you like best?

The Dandelion got its name from the French *dents de lion* meaning lion's teeth. Other names for it are Devil's Milk Pail, Shepherd's Clock and Golden Sun. Which of these names suits it best? Can you think of a *new* name for it?

Here are some more interesting names:

buttercup

yellow wagtail

giant crane fly *or* daddy-long-legs

lords and ladies

snapdragon

love-lies-bleeding

peacock

 Write down the names of each of the plants and creatures and say **how** you think it got its name. For example, you might write 'Lords and ladies got its name because it is so tall and elegant'.

Invent some new names for these species. Perhaps they remind you of something or have a special shape or colour. Draw a picture of them with their new names underneath.

Now quite rare; hunts by night for mice and rats; lives around farms. It is 34 cm from top to tail.

Usual name – Barn Owl.

Normally has between two and seven spots; flies; feeds on other little insects; 5–6 mm long.

Usual name – Ladybird.

Found throughout Britain, hibernates in muddy pond bottoms. Catches flies with its long tongue. Up to 10 cm long.

Usual name – Common Frog.

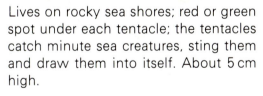

Lives on rocky sea shores; red or green spot under each tentacle; the tentacles catch minute sea creatures, sting them and draw them into itself. About 5 cm high.

Usual name – Beadlet Anemone.

Grows in cornfields and waste ground; used to commemorate men killed in war. Up to 60 cm tall.

Usual name – Poppy.

Extra Idea

Think of any other plants or creatures that live near you. Draw them and, underneath, write their real names and also new invented names. (Refer to a nature book or encyclopaedia if you need to.)

The Diver

Imagine what it is like to swim along the bottom of the ocean.

This is how the scientist Conrad Lorenz described it:

My childhood dream of flying is realized...

I glide over fairy-tale scenery...

The number of fish increases rapidly; dozens shoot from under me...

...a beautiful butterfly-fish in its dwelling under a capsized landing stage.

...needle fish, swift as arrows... grey-green snappers loitering... and the delightful blue and yellow striped grunts.

I now realize that I am rather cold... and climb the coral wall into the warm air and golden sun.

Library Research

Look in reference books and encyclopaedias for pictures of creatures and plants under the sea. Look carefully at the colours and shapes. Make **notes** on four or five different species; note their names and what they look like.

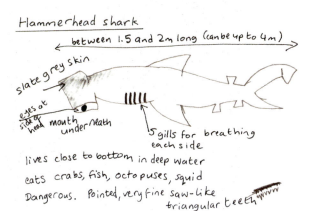

Imagine you are the diver in the picture and can see the things that you made notes about.

Write a story about it. Ask yourself: why am I diving? What can I see? How do I feel as I look at it?

Use the information you collected from the library books to write your story. The reader must be able to imagine what it is like under the sea – both the beauty and the danger.

> **Notes**
>
> You make notes to help you to remember things.
> > They can be in your quickest handwriting – as long as you can read them.
> >
> > You can cross out and alter things as much as you like.
> >
> > You need not write in complete sentences. Just jot down a few words.

Riddles

Riddles are puzzles. They describe something in an unusual way – but leave you to guess what it really is.

Here are two riddles written by two London school children. The pictures make it easy to guess what they are.

Hungry Thing
This thing is always hungry
it has a big mouth that gobbles big and small things up
but spits them out.
It goes to sleep
but in the morning it
starts to gobble things again.

By Chi-Quen Chiu.

It sinks in the ground.

Is red and yellow and orange.

It rises up again.

These two are more difficult. Turn them upside down to read the right answer.

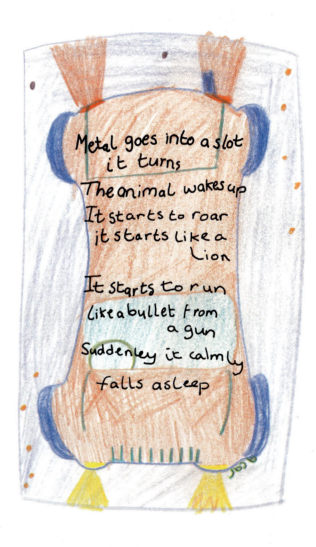

 Now you write a riddle.

First choose a subject. It could be one of these: a kettle, a washing machine, a hair dryer or a snail.

In draft, write down what it really does and what it looks like. Then think what it **reminds** you of.

Write your description as a riddle. Don't make it too easy for people to guess what it is.

'Bats' Teeth

A boy went to the dentist and didn't like it. Read the poem that he wrote.

The Drill

I hate the shivery drill
It is like bats' teeth
Nibbling away.
I hate the dentist's light
It is like lightning
Flashing down.
The dentist's white coat
Is like a ghost.
It is as if the ghost is coming to eat me.
He has his knife and fork.
I am stuck on a plate.

Gary Lewis (9)

Which lines do you think are good? Why?

He has told us what everything **reminded** him of. Was there really a bat nibbling him? Was there really a ghost? Was he really stuck to a plate? Or were they just things that he thought of as he sat in the dentist's chair?

Choose **one** of these things to write a poem about:

Walking alone in the dark.

A street full of noisy traffic.

A caged animal or bird.

The slide or swings in a park.

First, in rough, **make a simple list** of things that you **see** and **hear**. Then go over your list adding ideas about what each of the sights and sounds **reminds** you of.

For example, you might have written 'dark trees' on your list; these might remind you of giant black birds watching you. The sound of a passing motorbike might remind you of a lion's roar.

Use your list to **make a draft copy** of your poem. When you are happy with it, **copy it out** in your best handwriting to show to other people.

Rules of the Game

 Imagine you have bought a game called **Schooldays**. Unfortunately, when you open the box, the only thing you find is the board. There are no instructions, no penalty or bonus cards, no dice and no counters.

Look carefully at the board and try to work out how to play the game.

1. When you have understood the game, **write out a set of instructions**.

   You should make a draft copy first. Here are some questions to help you:

   How many can play?
   What do you need to play the game?
   How do you start?
   What are bonus and penalty cards? When do you pick them up and what do you do with them?
   How do you win?

2. Make some **bonus** and **penalty cards**. How many do you need? You can make them funny. What are you going to use instead of a dice? What will you use for counters?

3. Show the draft copy of your instructions to a friend to see whether he or she can understand them. Have you missed anything out? Are they completely clear?

4. Revise your instructions if necessary then copy them out neatly.

5. Now you can **play the game** at home or at school. Good luck with it!

Extra Ideas

Invent a new game to play in the park or playground, using:

    a bouncy ball, and a pair of roller skates and bat for each player,
or a heavy ball and a long flat piece of wood,
or some chalk that you can use on the ground and some small stones,
or some string and a balloon.

Write out the instructions.

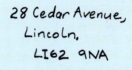

Choose one of the arguments and decide whose side you are on.

In rough, make a list of all the reasons why you agree with it.

Now **write a letter** explaining what you think:

to the Park Keeper (about cycling),
or to your class teacher (about fighting),
or your Head (about uniform),
or to a newspaper (about smoking).

Remember to lay your letter out correctly like this:

> 28 Cedar Avenue,
> Lincoln.
> LI62 9NA
>
> 17th February 1993
>
> Dear Sir,
>
> I think it is very unfair that people are not allowed to ride bicycles through the park. The road around the park is very dangerous and I am not allowed to cycle on it. This means I am often late for school because I have to wheel my bike.
>
> If ~~you~~ made part of the path through the park into a cycle track it would be safer for everybody.
>
> Yours faithfully,
>
> James Saunders

address

post code

date

start **Dear Sir** or **Dear Madam** to a person you don't know

or **Dear ...** (the person's name if you know it);

end **Yours sincerely** if it is somebody whose name you know

or **Yours faithfully** if you don't know the person's name

or **With love from** if it is a friend.

Extra Ideas

1 Read each other's letters and reply to the ones you don't agree with.

2 Think of another issue that you could write a letter about. For example, should animals be kept in cages? Should we give more money to poor countries? Are school holidays too long? Decide who to write to about it.

The Prayer of the Little Ducks

If animals could say prayers, what do you think they would ask for?

Dear God,
give us a flood of water.
Let it rain tomorow and always.
Give us plenty of little slugs
and other luscious things to eat.
Protect all folk who quack
and everyone who knows how to swim.

Amen

Carmen Bernos de Gasztold

Make up a prayer for one of these:

> a cat   a fox   a squirrel
> a fly   a shark   a bumble bee
>
> or any other animal you can think of.

You must think carefully what the creature would really like to ask God for.

Copy your prayer out beautifully, with a decorative border and a little picture of the creature.

Now choose a completely different sort of creature and make up another prayer. For example, if you wrote about a lion before, you could now write about a mouse or a rabbit.

Daydreams

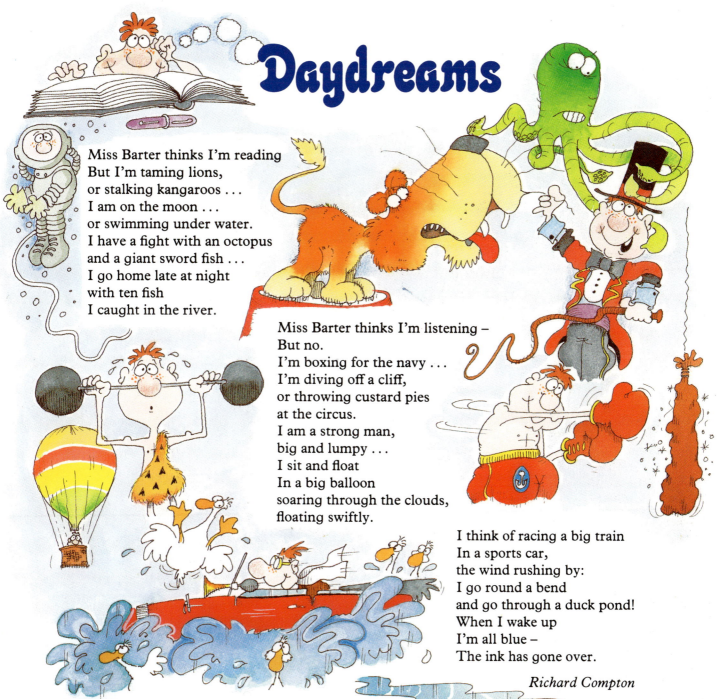

Miss Barter thinks I'm reading
But I'm taming lions,
or stalking kangaroos ...
I am on the moon ...
or swimming under water.
I have a fight with an octopus
and a giant sword fish ...
I go home late at night
with ten fish
I caught in the river.

Miss Barter thinks I'm listening –
But no.
I'm boxing for the navy ...
I'm diving off a cliff,
or throwing custard pies
at the circus.
I am a strong man,
big and lumpy ...
I sit and float
In a big balloon
soaring through the clouds,
floating swiftly.

I think of racing a big train
In a sports car,
the wind rushing by:
I go round a bend
and go through a duck pond!
When I wake up
I'm all blue –
The ink has gone over.

Richard Compton

Do you ever daydream that:

    you are an amazing fighter or dancer or explorer or athlete?
    you are so popular that everybody wants to be your friend?
    you have a wonderful tame animal that walks round with you?
    or something else?

Now **write a poem** about your Daydreams

Paragraphs

Look at these two pages. Which looks easier to read?

This is a solid mass of words. It looks boring, doesn't it?

This is broken up into short sections called **paragraphs**. It looks easier to read, doesn't it?

Paragraphs split up a page of writing to make it easier to read.

The Ship of Bones

In the days when sailing ships crossed the oceans, blown by the winds, there was one ship that all sailors dreaded to see. It was called the Ship of Bones. Its sails were deathly white and its figurehead was a skull and all along its length were carved the names of drowned sailors, and they say that the hull was made from their bones.

This story is the story of the only man who went aboard the Ship of Bones and lived to tell the tale. His name was Stoker, Bill Stoker, and he sailed on the ship *Mayfly*, that left Portsmouth on 1 June 1784...

They hadn't been gone more than a week when they were caught in a storm... in a terrible storm. The waves towered up six times as high as the mainmast, and the little ship was tossed about the ocean like a bit of cork in the foam. One moment it was rising up the head of a mighty wave and the next minute it was dashed down into the trough, and the waters blotted out the sun and it all went still, until another wave crashed down on her bows.

Well, the storm raged on for four days and four nights, and on the fourth night the sailors had given themselves up as good as dead. Their sails were in shreds, the rudder was broken, and half the crew were lying sick in their hammocks or being tossed across the cabin by the force of the sea.

Old Bill Stoker was lying in his bunk, thinking this would be his last night on this earth, when he heard a cry from up on deck, and this sailor comes running down to the cabin as white as a sheet.

"It's the Ship of Bones!" he cries. "We've had it now for sure, mates!"

1st paragraph describes the ship.

2nd paragraph introduces the hero.

3rd paragraph describes the storm.

4th paragraph describes the damage.

5th paragraph – a cry is heard.

6th paragraph – somebody speaks.

Now you write a story using paragraphs. It can be about *one* of these:

Discovered talent!

Imagine that one day you realise that you are brilliant at something. Perhaps it is singing, or playing tennis, or writing television commercials, or training animals... Do you become famous?

Write a story using paragraphs, like this:

1st paragraph   You are doing something and realise that you are very good at it. What do you think and say?

2nd paragraph   You practise hard at it. What is it like? How do you feel?

3rd paragraph   A stranger notices what you are doing. What does he or she say?

Carry on with the story using paragraphs at each new stage in the story.

The Cry of the Banshee

Banshees are horrible woman ghosts who can be heard crying and wailing in the night when someone is about to die. They have only one nostril, one fang tooth and webbed feet.

Write a frightening story about how you met a banshee. Arrange it in paragraphs like this:

1st paragraph   Describe what you were doing one evening. Maybe you were sitting comfortably at home. Or perhaps you were walking home.

2nd paragraph   You hear a strange cry. What does it sound like? How do you feel?

3rd paragraph   What happens next?

Carry on with the story using paragraphs.

Choose a Character

Here are some characters from famous books.

Try writing your own story about **one** of the characters. Remember to use paragraphs.

Later you might like to read the book and compare your stories.

Sid, from **The Battle of Bubble and Squeak** by Philippa Pearce.

Sid is an ordinary boy, with one ordinary wish – to keep a pet. Unfortunately, his mother *hates* animals, and won't have them in the house.

What is Sid to do? He secretly keeps two gerbils, called Bubble and Squeak, hidden in the toolshed. Will his mother find them? If so, what will she do? What will *he* do? You can expect a lot of trouble!

Write your own version of the story about a secret pet. (You can change Sid into a girl if you like, or alter his name, and he needn't keep gerbils.)

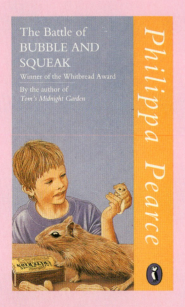

Annabel, from **Freaky Friday** by Mary Rodgers

A very extraordinary thing happened to Annabel. She explains:

"When I woke up this morning, I found I'd turned into my mother. There I was in my mother's bed, with my feet reaching all the way to the bottom, and my father sleeping in the other bed. I had on my mother's nightgown, and a ring on my left hand, I mean her left hand, and lumps and pins all over my head." She spent the whole day being her mother.

Imagine what would happen if you turned into your mother or father.

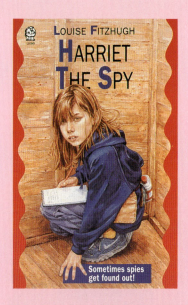

Harriet, from **Harriet the Spy** by Louise Fitzhugh

Harriet wants to be a famous writer when she grows up. This means she must learn all she can about grown-ups and how they behave.

She spies on people through windows and keyholes and writes it all down in her notebook.

What interesting things do you think Harriet might discover? What would she do if she spied on a grown-up doing something terrible?

Write a story about Harriet. You can change her name to your own if you like.

Titles

You can *either* choose a title before you start, *or* you can leave a space and add it afterwards.

An interesting title will make people want to read your story. Look at books in the library to give you ideas.

Some are the names of people: *Super Gran, Heidi, Fanny and the Monsters*.

Others are names of things or places: *The Secret Garden, George's Marvellous Medicine*.

Some tell you what happens: *The Runaway Summer, Hurricane, The Ghost on the Hill*.

Book Reviews

Reviews are a way of telling people:
   what you think a book is about,
   what you like about it,
   what you don't like about it.
Read these reviews of some very famous books.

Pollyanna by E. H. Porter

This is a story about a girl called Pollyanna who helps people. Her aunt, who she is staying with, is very strict.

  Miss Harrington was one of my favourite characters because Pollyanna would never come to her when she was asked – which made her very furious. My other favourite character was the dog.

  I loved this book because it gave me some idea about what it was like a long time ago. Some parts of the story are very funny but some are quite sad.

  Pollyanna taught all her village a game in which you were made glad. It shows that if you have a sad village you can change their lives. That was what the book was about.

Jane Hindley (10)

Danny the Champion of the World by Roald Dahl

This book is all about a boy called Danny and his father. Their big secret was that they poach in Mr Hazell's land. Danny invented a new way to poach pheasants by giving them sleeping pills. But they all flew away.

  My favourite character was the doctor. He was so merry and jolly and could keep secrets and not even tell his very own wife.

  The book was interesting to me because it was all about poaching. Before I had read the book I had never heard the word before! Also it was very good that the story started off with Danny as a baby. I felt as if I was part of the story, and this made me enjoy the book more.

Emma Holden (10)

Tom's Midnight Garden by Philippa Pearce

The main character is a boy called Tom who goes to stay with his aunt in a large old house. One night he goes into the back garden and travels back in time and meets a little girl who thinks he is a ghost.

I have tried to be fair with myself about reading this book. I found myself saying I liked it but I did find it difficult.

The first five chapters or so were all right but the middle of the book became confusing. It was not until the last few chapters that the authoress began to explain what had been happening.

If you intend to read this book, my advice is to read it in long bits at a time because otherwise you might get muddled up.

Alan Rose (11)

Have you read any of the books reviewed here?

If so, do you agree with what the reviewer says?

If not, does it make you want to read the book?

Write a review of a book that you have read.

Make sure you tell us:
   what sort of person the main character is;
   the most interesting thing that happens;
   anything you specially liked;
   anything you did not like.

Extra Idea

You can make a class display of your reviews to help people to decide which book to read next.

New Fantastic Chocochips!

A company invented a new chocolate bar called Chocochips and their advertising department had to make up a catchy jingle to help sell it. It had to be short, funny and rhyming.

They started by writing down as many ideas as they could.

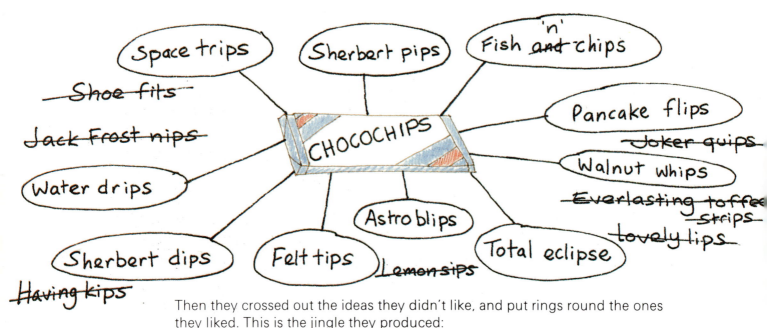

Then they crossed out the ideas they didn't like, and put rings round the ones they liked. This is the jingle they produced:

Do you think people will like this jingle? Does it make sense? Does this matter?

Imagine you are an advertiser. You have been asked to think up a catchy jingle for some new sweets called CANDY GLOWS (but you can change this name if you like).

Make a rough list of phrases which rhyme with Candy Glows. Decide which ones you will use and make them into your finished jingle.

Write out your jingle and design an eye-catching advertisement.

Extra Ideas

1 Design a wrapper for Candy Glows. Remember that it has to stand out on the sweetshop shelf so that everybody notices it.

2 Invent another product – something to eat or play with or use in the house. Think of a name for it and then advertise it.

3 Make a display of your advertisements. Which ones do you like? Why? Do any of them really tell us anything *true* or *useful* about the product? Does this matter?

Slang

 What would this boy's teacher **prefer** him to have said?

Why **doesn't** the musician say this?

"Ladies and gentlemen, I would like to perform for you a beautiful song called..."

What would this newspaper say if it used Standard English? Why doesn't it do so?

Would you be a bit surprised if you read this sentence in a school history book? Why?

Standard English: the language normally used in books. It is spoken when people wish to be clearly understood outside their own family and friends.

Slang: non-standard words and phrases, often used in conversation, on the radio and television, and so on.

1 Do you think it matters if you use slang:
   – if you are a disc jockey? Why?
   – if you are applying for an office job? Why?
   – if you are with friends going off to watch a match? Why?
   – if you are writing about a scientific experiment? Why?
   – if you are writing a story and you are telling us what the characters really said? Why?

2 Make a list of slang words meaning:
   food   steal
   a coward   someone who is clever
   money   hello!
   someone who is stupid   goodbye!

3 **Make up a conversation** between two children (or grown-ups) who are planning to go out together to visit or do something special.

Remember, the slang should be in their **speech**. You should use Standard English when you are telling the main story.

Crazy Machines

Look at this picture by the artist Heath Robinson:

What is the machine doing?

Can you see how it works?

Do you think it really could work?

Read this explanation of how it operates:

The machine is to enable a fat gentleman who cannot swim to cross the Channel. There is a large light air balloon. From it hangs a rope hooked on to the man's swimming costume to stop him sinking. Fixed under the balloon is an engine with a propellor which drives the whole thing forward.

If he wants to help, he can pull a rope which rings a bell. If he is hungry he can pull another rope and his dinner and a bottle of wine are lowered by a pulley.

Can you explain the other things on the machine?

Now you invent a machine which can do **one** of these things.

Wake you up gently at exactly 7:30 each morning.
Exercise your dog without having to go out of doors.
Peel the potatoes.

First make a draft copy, to work out exactly how it works. Then copy it out carefully.

Write an explanation of how it works. Again, you'll have to make a draft copy first.

Extra Ideas

Here are some more Heath Robinson machines. They might give you ideas either for new inventions of your own, or for a story about someone who invents crazy machines.

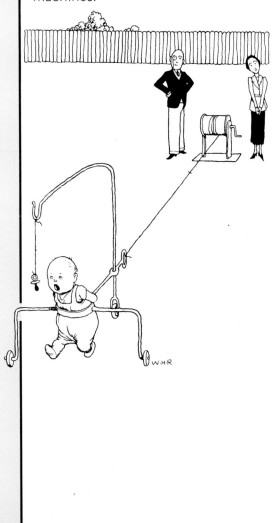

Who'll Look After Us?

Below it has been written out like a story. Read this new version.

Notice that we start a new paragraph every time a different person begins to speak.

David speaks	"I wish Mum would come back soon," said David. "Do you think she's all right?"
Jenny speaks	"Stop fussing," said Jenny. "She's often as late as this." Just then, they heard their mother coming in the front door.
David speaks	"Mum!" shouted David, running over to her.
Jenny speaks	"Are you all right?" asked Jenny anxiously.
Mum speaks	"I'm sorry I've been so long," said their Mum. "I want to talk to you both." The children sat down close to her. "Listen, I've got some bad news. I've just seen the doctor. They're going to operate on my knee and I'll be in hospital for about ten days."

Jenny speaks	"Oh Mum! How horrible for you!" cried Jenny.
David speaks	"Who'll look after us?" David asked.
Jenny speaks	"We don't need anybody," said Jenny. "I'll take charge."
Mum speaks	"No," said Mum. "I've arranged for somebody special to come and be here with you."

Notice also that each new paragraph is **indented**. That means that it starts a little way in from the left hand margin. If you look through other stories in books you will see that it is always done like that.

 Now you write a story.

Imagine what would happen if the grown-ups in your home had to be away. (Perhaps it has happened to you?) Who would look after you? How would you manage? Describe what happens. Remember to include plenty of speech.

Direct Speech

When people speak in stories, remember:
   their actual words go into speech marks "...";

start a new paragraph whenever a different person starts speaking;

indent new paragraphs a couple of centimetres from the margin.

A Map of the Feelings

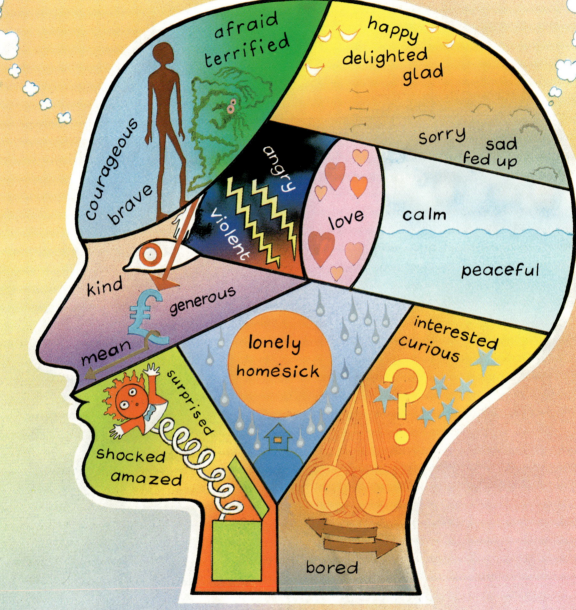

 Look at this 'map' of your feelings. You probably have all these different feelings from time to time.

Think about each one in turn.

When have you felt very calm and peaceful? Think of a special occasion.

When do you feel particularly sad or fed up? Is there something that always upsets you?

What makes you very angry? Think of some really annoying thing.

Read this poem. Why do you think that it is called *The Four Winds*?

The Four Winds

Sad –

    Pouring rain washing faces,
    Tears held back.
    My fingers held wet soil
    reluctant to throw.

Anger –

    He said I was his best friend,
    The pig!
    Playing with Tony, our den,
    hours of weaving straw into the roof.
    Smashed by that pig!

Excitement –

    Standing cold, bare feet, pyjamas,
    Hands trembling, teasing
    Will I? Won't I?
    I'm going!

Lonely –

    Walking round the cinder playground
    watching.
    Everyone's big, everyone's got pals,
    except me.
    Playtime and cinders go on for ever.

Chris McIllroy

 In rough jot down a few words or phrases about some of the feelings on the map. Describe when you felt like that.

Now use these notes to **write a poem**. Some of the lines could start like this:

    I feel lonely when . . .
    I feel excited when . . .
or,
    Lonely –
    . . . .

Myself and Other People

 Write a story about yourself and your friends on **one** of the subjects below:

1 A Good Time

Write about a time when you really enjoyed yourself. Where were you? Who with? Remember exactly what people said and did and how you felt.

2 Feeling Left Out

Being left out of a game or a conversation isn't much fun. It can make you very sad or angry.

Write about a time when you felt left out.

> **Remember:**
> Include plenty of conversation, trying to show exactly how your friends really talk.
>
> You can change people's names if you want to.
>
> Try to make it as true as possible.

3 The Things We Saw

Remember a time when you saw an unusual thing or person. Maybe it was on a school outing. Who were you with? What did you think when you saw it? What was it like?

4 It Isn't Fair!

Remember a time when you, or a friend, got into trouble and you didn't think it was fair.

How did it start? Who were you with? What did people say? How did you feel? How did other people feel?

Survival

 Kate and Joseph have been shipwrecked on a beautiful tropical island. Luckily they are quite clever at working out how to survive and look after themselves.

How did they light a fire without matches?

Kate knew how to do this. Here are her instructions. Can you understand them? You may have to look up some words in a dictionary.

1. Choose a <u>clear</u> windless position.

2. Collect very dry fragments of dead wood dust, dead grass, fluff from pockets and other dry material to use as <u>tinder</u>.

3. Collect little dead twigs for <u>kindling</u> and larger sticks to burn later.

4. Find a lump of flint and strike with a steel blade to make sparks

or strike two lumps of <u>quartz</u> together.

5. As sparks land on the tinder, <u>blow</u> very gently till a flame <u>appears</u>. Add the kindling, then firewood.

6. Make sure the fire cannot spread to other places such as near trees and plants or your hut.

How did they build their hut?

You make up some instructions. You can do it with pictures if you like drawing. You should make a draft copy first, then it doesn't matter if you make mistakes or alterations.

Remember

They have an axe and some rope. There are lots of palm trees.

The hut must be strong enough to withstand strong winds and rain in a tropical storm.

It needs to be comfortable inside.

Your instructions can start like this:

1 Choose a growing palm tree to act as a support.
2 Chop down . . .

How did they prepare their food?

Joseph was the expert cook. This picture shows him cooking a fish. Can you explain in your own words how he did it?

How did they build a raft to escape on?

You make up some instructions. The raft must be strong enough for rough seas. The palm leaves might be useful. How will they make it go in the right direction?

Extra Ideas

Make up instructions for making smoke signals or trapping a wild animal or making fresh pineapple juice.

The Captain's Diary

The captain of a sailing ship kept this diary of a voyage from Russia to England. It was the last voyage he was ever to make...

6 July – We took a cargo of silver sand and fifty large boxes of earth. We set sail at noon, followed by a fresh east wind. There are nine people on board: five sailors, two mates, a cook and myself as captain.

13 July – The crew are unhappy for some reason. They seemed scared but will not say why.

14 July – I am worried about the crew. The mate asked them what was wrong. They would not answer and made the sign of the cross. The mate lost his temper and hit one of them. I expected to see a fight but the men did nothing. It is very strange.

16 July – One of the crew is missing. Nobody can explain this. The men are more frightened than ever. They say that there is something other than the cargo on board!

17 July – One of the men came to my cabin today. He was trembling with fear. He told me there was a strange man on board the ship. While he was on watch, he had sheltered behind the deck-house during a rainstorm. A tall thin man had come up the steps, walked along the deck and vanished. The sailor was so frightened I decided to have the ship searched. I wanted to stop a panic.

We made a thorough search of the ship but found nothing.

29 July – Another loss. The second mate has disappeared. The men are in a panic. We are all going to arm ourselves. We have run into storm, and are all tired. Another man lost during a storm.

30 July – We are getting nearer to England. All our sails are set. I went to sleep as I was too tired to keep going. The mate woke me. He told me that both the man on watch and the steersman are missing. There are now only myself, the mate and two hands left to work the ship.

1 August – We have had two days of fog. Not a sail could be seen. We are in the English Channel, so had hoped to get help from another ship. But the fog prevented this. I do not know what is going to happen to us.

2 August, midnight – I was woken up by a cry and rushed on deck. I met the first mate. He tells me another man has gone. Lord help us! The mate says we are now in the North Sea. The fog seems to move with us. Only God can now help us – and God seems to have left us.

3 August – At midnight I went to see the man at the wheel. When I got to it there was nobody there. I grabbed the wheel and shouted for the mate. He came rushing on deck and I could see that he had gone mad.

"I'm sure It is here," he said. "I know It now. I saw It last night. It was tall and thin and pale like a ghost. It was at the front of the ship looking out. I crept behind It. I stabbed with my knife, but the knife went clean through It." As he spoke, he took out his knife and waved it in front of my face.

"But I know It is here," he went on. "I'll find It. It is in one of the boxes. I'll open them one by one. You work the wheel and leave it to me." Then he went below. I saw him come out on deck again with a tool chest and a lamp. He is mad! He is stark raving mad. It is no use me trying to stop him!

Moments later I heard a scream which made my blood run cold. The mate came up on deck. He was a complete madman. His eyes rolled. His face was twisted with fear. "Save me! Save me!" he cried. He stared around at the fog. Then he looked at me and said, "He is there! I know the secret now. The sea will save me from him. You had better come too, Captain, before it is too late." Before I could say a word he had thrown himself into the sea.

I see it all now. It was this madman who had got rid of the men one by one. And now he has killed himself. God help me! How am I going to explain these things when I get to port? When I get to port! Will I ever get there?

4 August – The fog is still all around the ship. There must be a sun, but it cannot break through. Last night I saw him! God forgive me, but the mate was right to jump overboard. It is better to die like a man in the blue water. But I am a captain and a captain must not leave his ship. I will tie my hands to the wheel. I will hold on to the cross which he cannot dare to touch. I must save my soul and my honour as a captain. I am getting weaker. The night is coming again. If we are wrecked, this log book may be found. God and the saints save me from this Demon. Help a poor sailor who is trying to do his best. . . . (*End of the captain's diary.*)

Bram Stoker

Later the ship was found with the Captain dead, tied to the wheel. His diary was lying nearby.

What do *you* think really happened?

Imagine he managed to live for one more day. **Write his diary entry for 5 August**, describing clearly what he saw.

Extra Ideas

1 Imagine you go camping with a friend in a wild and deserted area. (Decide what part of the world it is.) **Write a diary of each day.** Probably you have a nice time for the first day or two; describe what you see and do. But then something unusual happens. Do you get lost? Do you meet somebody strange? Or do you get caught in a terrible storm or flood? Do you run out of food and have to hunt? How do you get back?

2 You are at home during the school holidays. Write your diary for two or three ordinary days; then you start thinking that there is a small strange creature hiding in your house, so the next diary entries tell how you tried to track it down.

The Loch Ness Monster

Loch Ness is a lake in Scotland, about 40 kilometres long and more than 200 metres deep. For hundreds of years people have thought that there is a great monster living under the water.

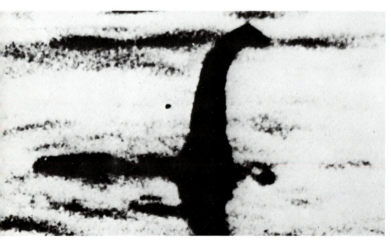

In 1934 Mr R. K. Wilson, a doctor from London, took this photograph of what seems to be a head and neck. But he never claimed that it was a monster.

In 1951 Mr Lachlan Stuart, a local woodman, took this photograph. He was getting up to milk his cow when he saw a shape in the water. He says it had a long neck and small head.

In 1977 Anthony Shiels took this photograph from the grounds of Urquhart Castle. He thought it was a neck, which appeared to be four or five feet long, but he couldn't see any eyes.

Do you think these photographs are genuine or could they be fakes?

Do you think there might really be a monster in Loch Ness? (People say it is a descendent of prehistoric creatures.)

If there is a monster would it breathe air or water? What would it eat?

Most important, why can't scientists and divers find it?

Invent a Monster which you think could be living in Loch Ness. Draw it. Show what it eats and where it lives. Has it got a mate?

Write a story with four chapters. You may want to illustrate each chapter.

Chapter 1: The Plan
Explain how you and your friend the Professor plan to find and catch the monster. (Maybe you could use dolphins to help, or go down in a glass capsule or use diving equipment.)

Chapter 2: The expedition
Describe how you go under water with the Professor and see the monster. What is it like? What does it do?

Chapter 3: Capture
Describe how you catch the monster.

Chapter 4: The End
Explain what you do. Do you kill the monster? Do you capture it alive? If so, what do you do with it? Do you let it go free again?

Research
Find a good book on dinosaurs and look up Plesiosaurus and Macroplata. Some scientists think that if the Loch Ness Monster exists it probably looks like one of these.

School Newspapers

It can be fun starting your own newspaper. There is a lot of hard work involved, so a large group of you need to do it together.

Before you start, get hold of some copies of the **real local newspaper** of your area.

Study it. See how it is laid out with headlines, picture captions, advertisements and so on.

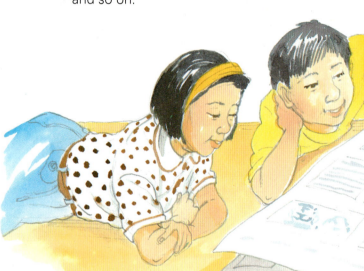

Jobs to be done

1 Think of a **name** for your newspaper.

2 Make a list of **items to include**:

– **Latest news**, such as a child winning a contest ('Year 6 boy is the champ!'), a dog comes into the playground ('Wild animal terrorises children'), a teacher gets engaged ('Mr Butler in holiday romance') or scratches her car ('Mrs Dexter in street drama'), a class visits the museum ('Year 6 meets the dinosaurs!') etc.

– **Interviews** with a teacher, an ex-pupil, the school caretaker. ('Did you know that he was a snooker fanatic and his wife had twins?') People love local gossip!

– **Articles**, poems, book or TV reviews, What the Stars Foretell and so on.

– **Letters** to the editor ('Dear Sir, I don't think it's fair that...').

– **Puzzles**, advertisements ('Baby gerbils need good home...' 'Old comics for sale...') cartoons and so on.

3 **Write and edit** the items:

– Decide who is to **write** each article. Tell them to do it **in draft form** at this stage.

– **Edit** each item as it comes in. Is it **interesting** enough? Is it too long or too short? How can it be improved? Does it need a picture?

– Plan exciting **headlines** which make people want to read on. They shouldn't be more than about five words long.

– If you have a **word processor** or a special computer program for newspaper layout then you can start typing it in.

SCHOOL MEALS SHOCK!

CLASS 4 IN NETBALL DRAMA

THE GREAT ESCAPE

– If you are not using a word processor, each article should be written on **strips of paper ten centimetres wide**, so that the columns are the same width. Paste them on a large sheet of paper and pin it up on a school notice board.

Writing for Little Children

Do you have a nursery or infant department in your school? Or do you have any little brothers or sisters or friends you could write for? Think what sort of picture books you could write for them.

Here are some examples.

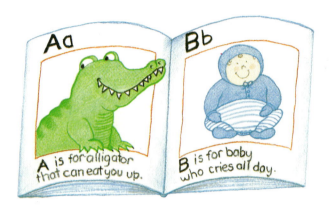

An ABC book

For 3- to 5-year-olds. Think of a really interesting word for every letter of the alphabet.

A simple fairy story

For 3- to 6-year-olds. Keep it very simple indeed. Little children like princesses, witches, monsters and animals that change into people.

Real life stories

A story about people and places that your readers really know. It can be funny.

An information book

This must be very simple indeed. It might be about animals or plants or transport or different places.

How to make a simple book

1 First make a draft copy. Plan the pictures you will put on each page and the words that go with them. For little children you only need one or two sentences on each page. Decide how many pages you need.

2 Check with your teacher that you have made no spelling mistakes.

3 Ask your teacher for some big sheets of paper. Fold them in half to make a book.

4 Write the words in really big print.

You might start writing in pencil and then go over it later with black pen or felt tip. You could write it on a word processor. Draw or stick in the pictures.

5 Draw or paint an attractive cover for it.

6 Try to arrange a time to read your book to some little children. See if they like it and can read it themselves.

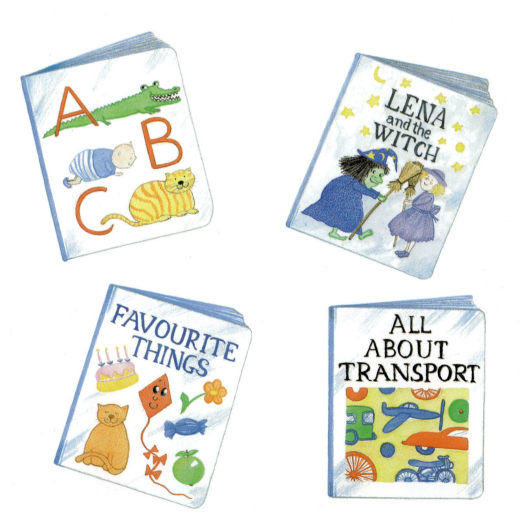